The Library of Living and Working in Colonial Times ™

A Day in the Life of a Colonial Dressmaker

Amy French Merrill

The Rosen Publishing Group's
PowerKids Press ™
New York

For Nene, whom I love and admire

Published in 2002 by The Rosen Publishing Group, Inc.
29 East 21st Street, New York, NY 10010

First Edition

Book Design: Danielle Primiceri
Layout Design: Maria E. Melendez and Nick Sciacca
Project Editor: Frances E. Ruffin

Photo Credits: Cover and title page, pp. 4, 7, 8, 11, 15, 16 © North Wind Pictures; p. 12 © The Granger Collection; p. 19 © Leif Skoogfors/CORBIS; p. 20 © Francis G. Mayer/CORBIS.

Merrill, Amy French.
  A day in the life of a colonial dressmaker / Amy French Merrill.
    p. cm. – (The Library of living and working in colonial times)
  ISBN 0-8239-5818-3
  1. Dressmaking—United States—History—eighteenth century—Juvenile
literature. 2. Dressmakers—United States—History—18th
century—Juvenile literature. [1. Dressmaking. 2. United
States—History—Colonial period, ca. 1600–1775.] I. Title. II. Series.
  TT504.4 .M47 2002
  646.4'00974'09032-dc21   00-01300

Contents

A Young Dressmaker

One beautiful morning in early June 1753, Bess O'Donnell looked out of the shop window at the rising sun. The cobblestone streets of Philadelphia, Pennsylvania, were busy with townspeople. Bess's grandparents had come to the **colony** of Pennsylvania from Ireland many years ago. Her grandfather and father were trained as weavers. Weavers are skilled workers who spin yarn into cloth. Bess worked with cloth, too. Since the age of 14, Bess had worked as an **apprentice** to learn the skills she would need to be a dressmaker.

◄ *In colonial times, young girls, like the one in this painting, learned to sew at an early age.*

Sewing Skills

Bess had been an apprentice for five years. Like many colonial girls, she began to sew at the age of four. By age 11, she could knit lace, spin thread and yarn, sew, weave, and make quilts. Bess saved examples of her sewing skills, such as fancy embroidery stitches, on a **sampler**. Other samplers showed practical sewing skills, such as making buttonholes. Girls and women seeking work as dressmakers used their samplers to show customers the work they could do.

This is an 1815 sampler sewed by a 10-year-old girl named Louisa Upham. ▶

The Milliner's Shop

When her time as an apprentice was over, Bess worked in one of the finest shops in Philadelphia! Mrs. MacDonald, a **milliner**, owned the shop. Items such as shirts, aprons, caps, cloaks, **shifts**, **petticoats**, and gloves were made and sold there. She also sold cloth, ribbons, pocketbooks, and hats. Bess was one of several dressmakers who worked there. Bess sewed clothes and waited on customers. As an apprentice, Bess had learned to read and do math. These were important skills for taking orders and keeping records.

◀ *This drawing shows a woman in the eighteenth-century buying cloth in a milliner's shop.*

A Port City

Philadelphia was one of the largest cities in the 13 colonies. It was on the Delaware River, not far from the Atlantic Ocean. Philadelphia was a **port** city. Its goods were **exported** and **imported** to and from Europe by ship. Mrs. MacDonald received goods and news about the world by ship. Sometimes she received a type of doll called a fashion baby. Fashion babies were dressed in the latest London styles and were sent from England to the colonies. Milliners used them as displays in their shops.

This is a 1756 map of Pennsylvania. ▶

Fashion in the Colonies

Cloth and clothing were expensive. As a dressmaker, part of Bess's job was to mend and update worn clothes. That way they lasted for many years. In colonial America, women and girls wore a type of long dress, called a gown, and a petticoat underneath. They wore a simple cap, which was covered by a hat when they went outdoors. Men and boys wore knee-length pants called breeches, a shirt, vest, and coat. Men and women wore stockings and low-heeled shoes. Men often wore wigs made of human, horse, or goat hair.

◀ *This tea party shows what women and men wore in the 1700s. It was important for dressmakers to keep up with the latest clothing styles.*

The Importance of Cloth

Bess helped Mrs. MacDonald set out items such as fans, purses, and **kerchiefs** in pleasing displays. Most items in the shop came from England or other parts of Europe. The colonies produced simple wool cloths and a sturdy fabric known as **linsey-woolsey**. Most colonists were not wealthy. They wore simple clothes made from cloth woven at home. Store-made clothes were bought and worn mostly by wealthy colonists living in cities. Customers could expect a made-to-order gown completed in one day.

This woman is spinning wool to make cloth. Cloth was the most expensive item sold in a milliner's shop. Luxury fabrics, such as silk, were shipped from other parts of the world. ▶

The Mantua Maker

When a customer came into the shop, Bess would say, "What do you buy?" This was the way colonial salespeople commonly greeted customers. Bess had a customer who was one of the city's most skilled dressmakers. She made the popular gowns called mantuas. These dresses had skirts that could be up to 18 feet (6 m) wide! They often were decorated with lace, feathers, ribbons, buttons, and embroidery, or designs stitched into the cloth. Bess held her breath as she measured and cut silk fabric for the mantua maker.

◀ *Only the richest women in the colonies could afford to have fine dresses made with lace, ribbons, and embroidery.*

The Liberty Bell

Bess went to the workroom to sew. As she stitched, she could hear Mrs. MacDonald talk with customers about the news of the day. One big event was getting a great bell ready to be hung in the State House, one of Philadelphia's public buildings. The bell had been made to honor William Penn, the founder of the colony of Pennsylvania. It was called the Liberty Bell. The bell had cracked when it was first rung months earlier. Two metal workers were repairing the bell to hang in the State House the next week.

The Liberty Bell hangs in Independence Hall in Philadelphia. ▶

The Legend of the Flag

Dressmaking was one of the few **trades**, or jobs, open to women in colonial times. A few women became quite famous for their sewing. One such woman was Betsy Ross. Betsy Ross and her husband had an **upholstery** business in Philadelphia during the 1700s. They also took in other sewing jobs, including flag making. According to **legend**, Betsy Ross knew a young general named George Washington. In the spring of 1776, General Washington asked her to make a flag. It became the first American flag.

◄ *The flag that Betsy Ross made had a design of stars and stripes, in the colors red, white, and blue.*

What the Future Holds

At the end of a long workday, Bess helped Mrs. MacDonald tidy up the shop. As they worked, Mrs. MacDonald told Bess about the growing conflict between England and France. Both countries had colonies in the eastern part of young America. They both claimed land in the West but did not agree on who owned the land. A fight was brewing. Bess wondered what the future of England's colonies would be. As Bess O'Donnell walked home, she yawned. There was one thing she knew for certain. Her future included another long day at the shop tomorrow!

Glossary

apprentice (uh-PREN-tis) A young person learning a skill or trade.

colony (KAH-luh-nee) An area in a new country where the people are still ruled by the leaders and laws of their old country.

exported (ek-SPORT-id) Goods sent to another place to be sold.

imported (im-PORT-id) Goods brought in from foreign countries.

kerchiefs (KER-chifs) Short scarves worn at the neck.

legend (LEJ-end) A story passed down that many people believe.

linsey-woolsey (LIN-zee WUL-zee) A fabric made from weaving linen and wool together.

milliner (MIH-lih-ner) A merchant who sold cloth, clothes, and clothing accessories.

petticoats (PEH-tee-kohts) Skirts worn under a gown, usually made of linen, wool, or cotton.

port (PORT) A city or town where ships come to dock and trade.

sampler (SAM-plur) A piece of cloth on which examples of different sewing skills are stitched.

shifts (SHIFTS) Long, shirtlike undergarments.

trades (TRAYDZ) Kinds of work that require special training.

upholstery (up-HOHL-stuh-ree) Heavy fabric used to make furniture.

Index

Web Sites:

To learn more about colonial dressmakers, check out this Web site:

www.history.org/life/clothing/intro/index.html